This book belongs to

Aa	Bb	Cc	Dd	Ee	Ff	Gg	Hh	Ii	Jj	Kk	Ll	Mm
Nn	Oo	Pp	Qq	Rr	Ss	Tt	Uu	Vv	Ww	Xx	Yy	Zz

How to use this book

Your child's name is usually one of the first words he/she will learn to recognize and learn how to spell. Learning how to write one's name is an essential skill that preschoolers and kindergarteners can do with practice. It is especially important to teach the correct letter formation before bad habits are formed. This book provides multiple opportunities to practice writing your child's name with guided letters and then with less support, so go through the pages sequentially.

<u>A few things to consider before using this book:</u>
- ✓ Can your child recognize his/her name in print?
- ✓ Can your child orally spell his/her name and recognize the letters by name?
- ✓ Is your child ready to grasp a writing tool functionally to write and draw?

<u>A few things to remember:</u>
- ✓ All children develop their fine motor skills at a different rate. Encourage independence with daily fine motor activities to develop hand muscles and dexterity.
- ✓ Small hands work better with smaller writing tools such as crayons or shorter pencils.
- ✓ Help your child find a functional grasp to comfortably hold the writing tool. The tripod grip is the ideal way to hold the writing tool.
- ✓ Teach your child how to hold the book or paper down in place with the non-dominant hand.
- ✓ Teach your child that names are read and written from left to right.
- ✓ Focus more on the correct letter formation than your child's print size and neatness.
- ✓ Name each letter and describe how the letters are formed as your child is writing them. Have your child say the letter and describe the way it is formed. (For example, for letter B say, "Start at the top and draw a straight line down. Lift your pencil and go back to the top and make a curve and then another curve to the bottom line.)
- ✓ Depending on your child's readiness or length of his/her name, consider focusing on one letter at a time.
- ✓ Teach your child that his/her name is always written the same way.

Change it up!

✓ Your child will learn to write his/her name when there are multiple opportunities to practice writing it.

✓ Encourage your child to use different writing tools such as pencils, colored pencils, and crayons when using this book.

✓ Encourage your child to label his/her room and belongings.

✓ Talk about other words that begin with the letters in your child's name.

✓ Tell your child the meaning of his/her name and why it was chosen.

✓ Count and compare how many letters are in your child's name and in other familiar names.

✓ Show and tell the importance of name writing and recognition in every day life.

✓ Provide opportunities for your child to practice writing and building his/her name in different ways while playing:

- Use Play Doh
- Use shaving cream
- Use chalk
- Use paint
- Use stickers
- Trace name in the sand
- Use dry erase markers on a white board
- Build your name with toys, letter beads, etc.

Encourage your child and help build confidence in writing his/her name. Working on a page or two each day should keep your child from frustration.

Enjoy!

How to Hold a Pencil

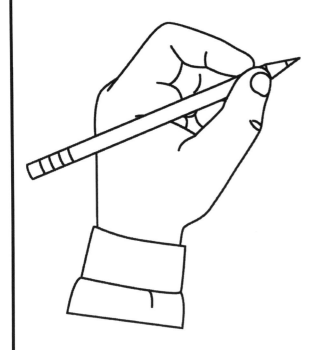 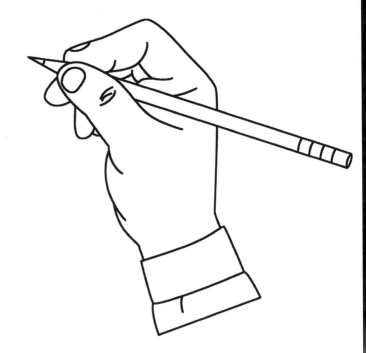

Left Hand

Right Hand

Use a tripod grip.

Read your name. Then say the letters in your name and use your fingers to trace each letter. Focus on how each letter is formed. Then use a crayon or pencil to trace your name from left to right.

My name is

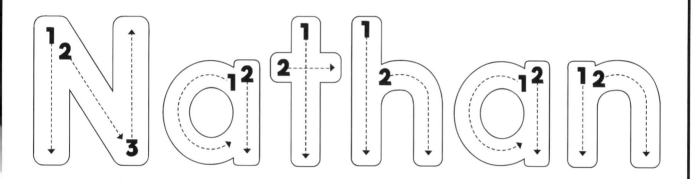

Trace the letters in your name.

Say each letter as you write it and focus on how each letter is formed.

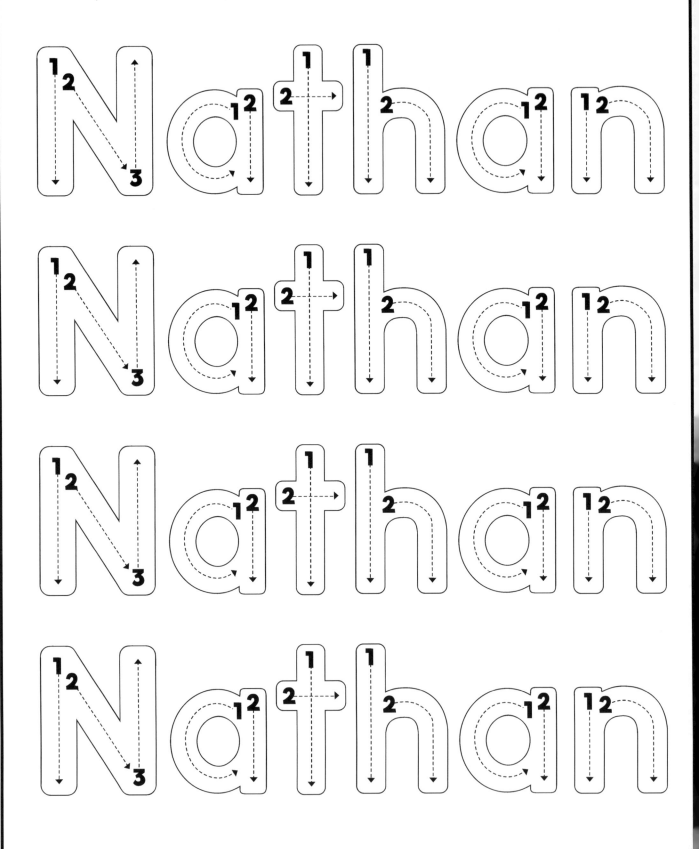

Trace the letters in your name.

Say each letter as you write it and focus on how each letter is formed.

Trace the letters in your name.

Say each letter as you write it and focus on how each letter is formed.

Trace the letters in your name.

Say each letter as you write it and focus on how each letter is formed.

Trace the letters in your name.

Say each letter as you write it and focus on how each letter is formed.

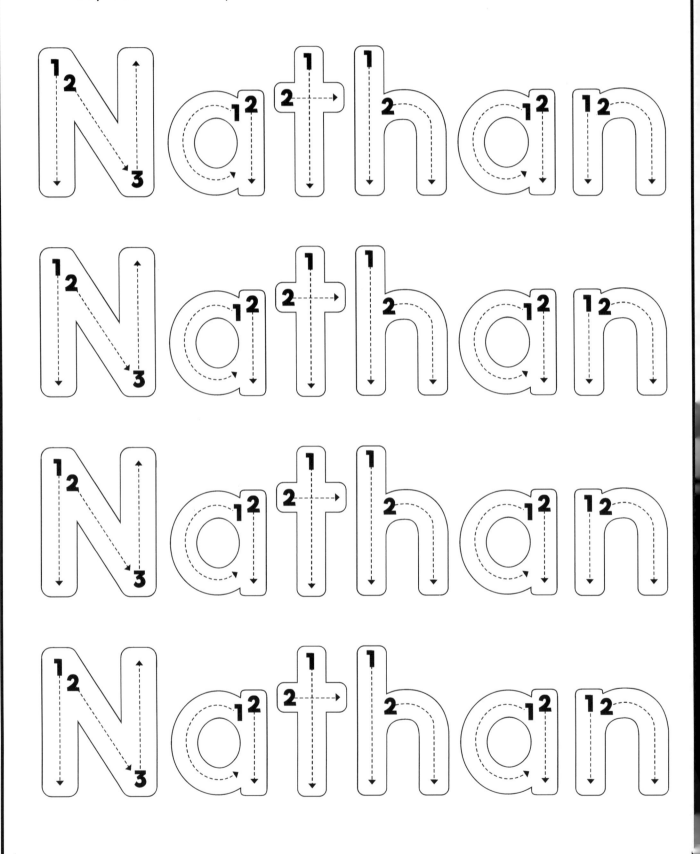

Trace the letters in your name.
Say each letter as you write it and focus on how each letter is formed.

Trace the letters in your name.

Say each letter as you write it and focus on how each letter is formed.

Trace the letters in your name.
Say each letter as you write it and focus on how each letter is formed.

Trace the letters in your name.

Say each letter as you write it and focus on how each letter is formed.

Trace the letters in your name.

Say each letter as you write it and focus on how each letter is formed.

Trace the letters in your name.

Say each letter as you write it and focus on how each letter is formed.

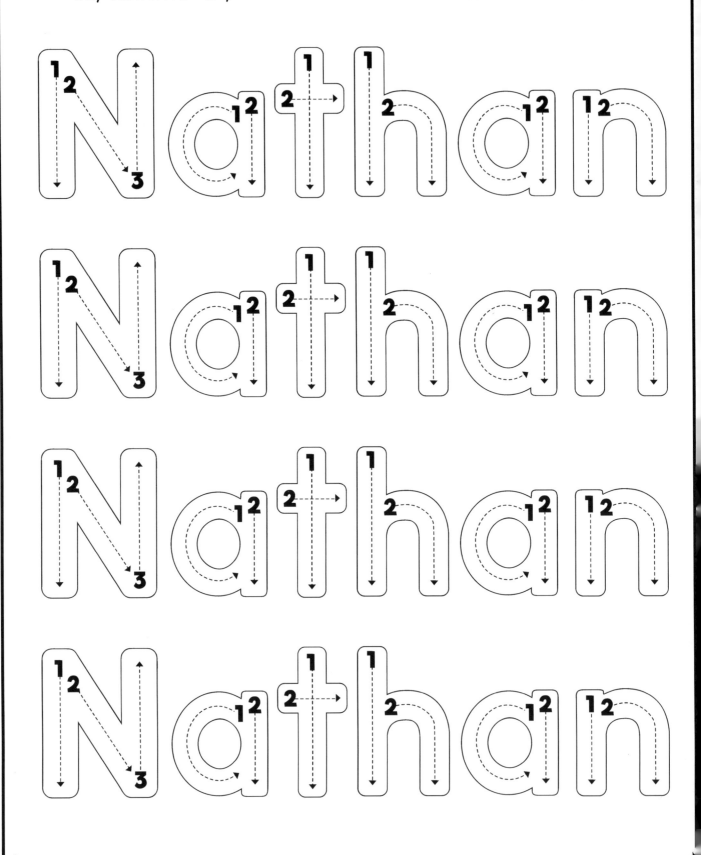

Trace the letters in your name.

Say each letter as you write it and focus on how each letter is formed.

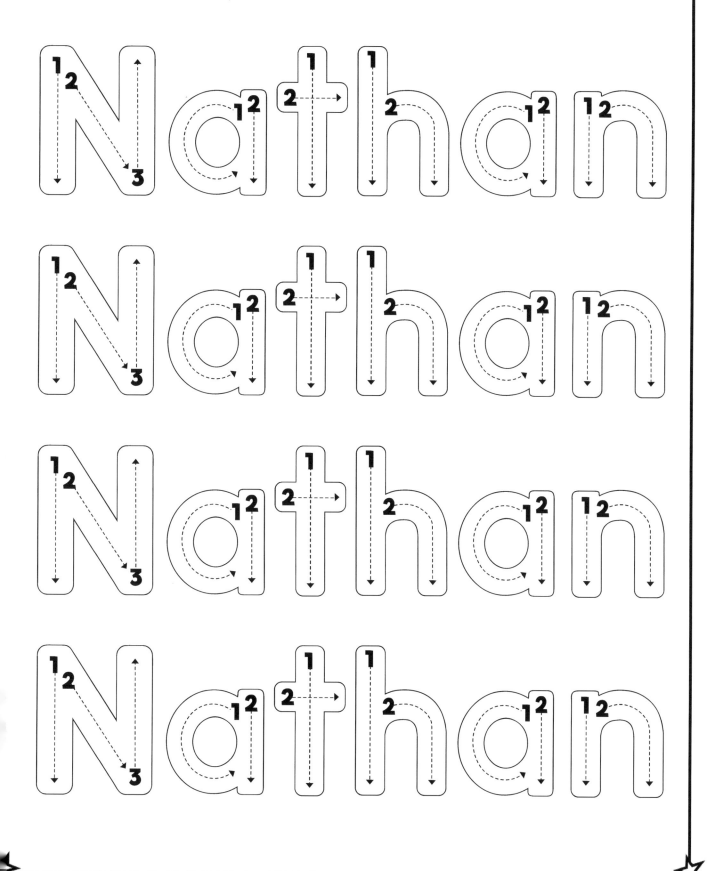

Trace the letters in your name.

Say each letter as you write it and focus on how each letter is formed.

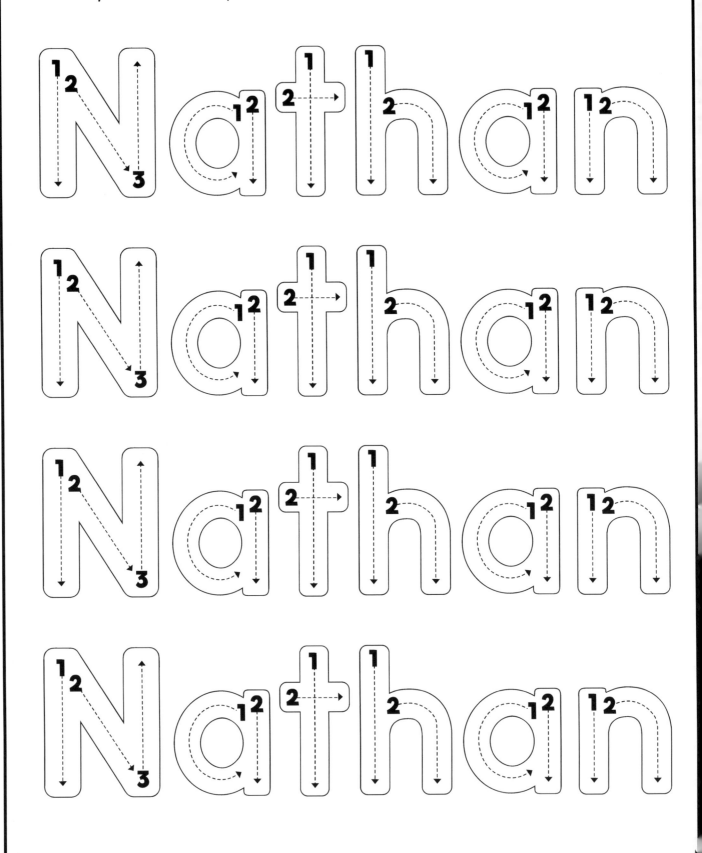

Trace the letters in your name.

Say each letter as you write it and focus on how each letter is formed.

Write your name inside the lines. Focus on how each letter is formed.

Nathan

Nathan

Nathan

Nathan

Write your name inside the lines. Focus on how each letter is formed.

Nathan

Nathan

Nathan

Nathan

Write your name inside the lines. Focus on how each letter is formed.

Nathan

Nathan

Nathan

Nathan

Nathan

Nathan

Nathan

Nathan

Write your name inside the lines. Focus on how each letter is formed.

Nathan

Nathan

Nathan

Nathan

Write your name inside the lines.

Nathan

Nathan

Nathan

Nathan

Nathan

Nathan

Write your name inside the lines.

Nathan

Nathan

Nathan

Nathan

Nathan

Nathan

Write your name inside the lines.

Nathan

Nathan

Nathan

Nathan

Nathan

Nathan

Write your name inside the lines.

Nathan

Nathan

Nathan

Nathan

Nathan

Nathan

Write your name inside the lines.

Nathan

Nathan

Nathan

Nathan

Nathan

Nathan

Trace your name. Say each letter as you write it.

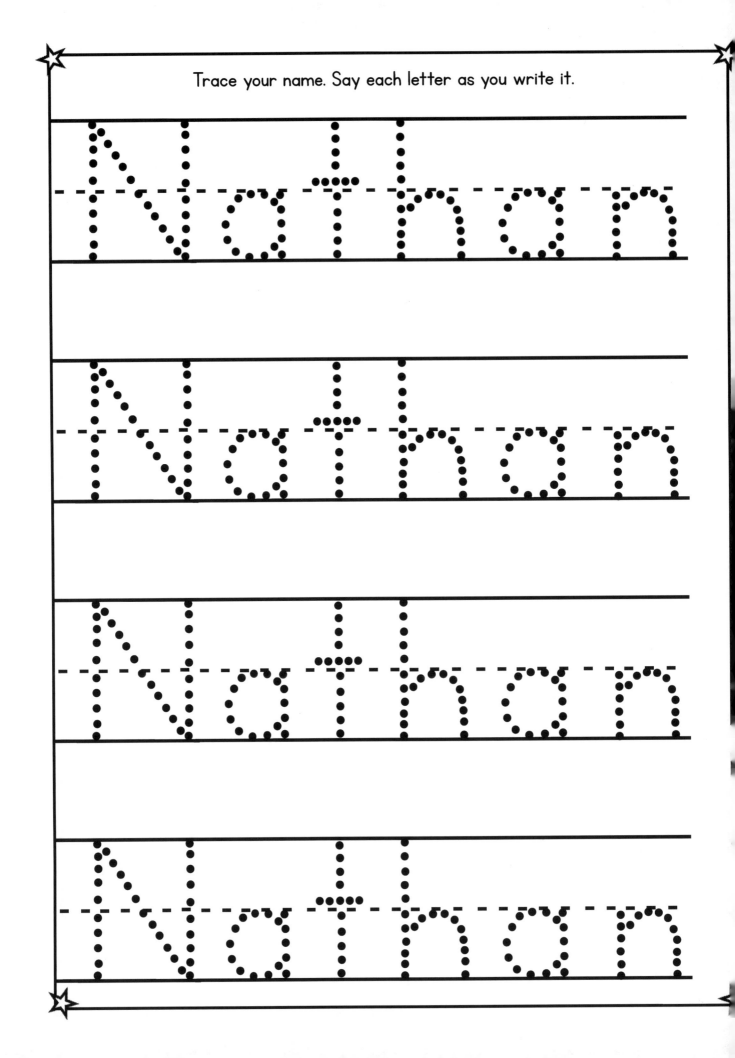

Trace your name. Say each letter as you write it.

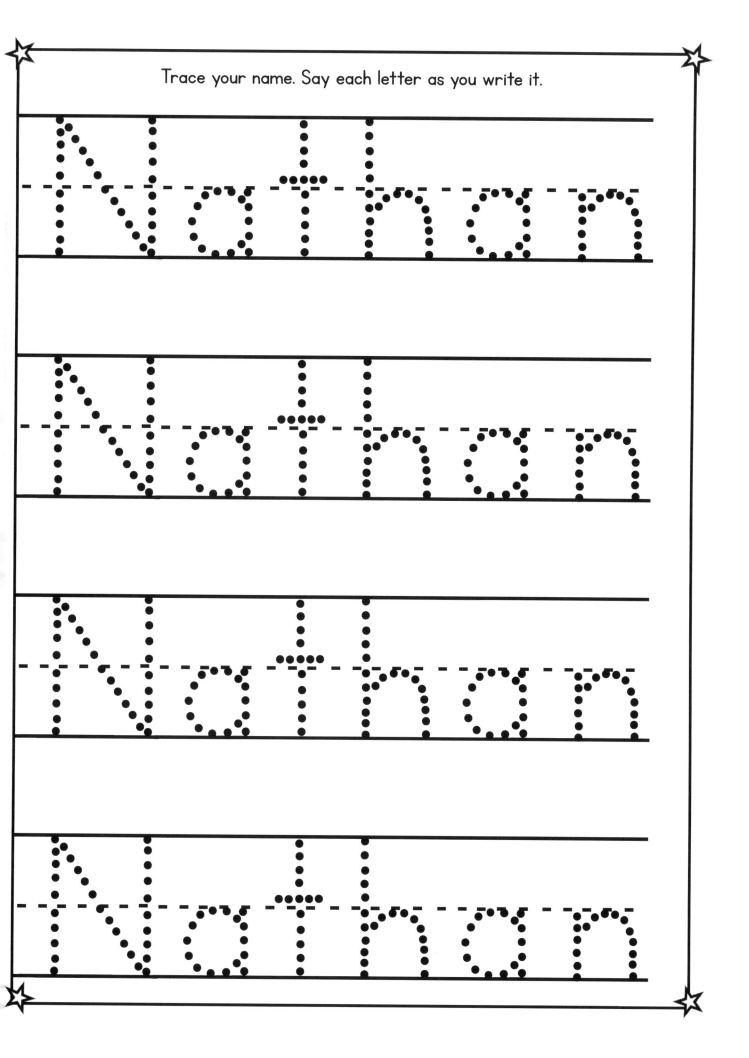

Trace your name. Say each letter as you write it.

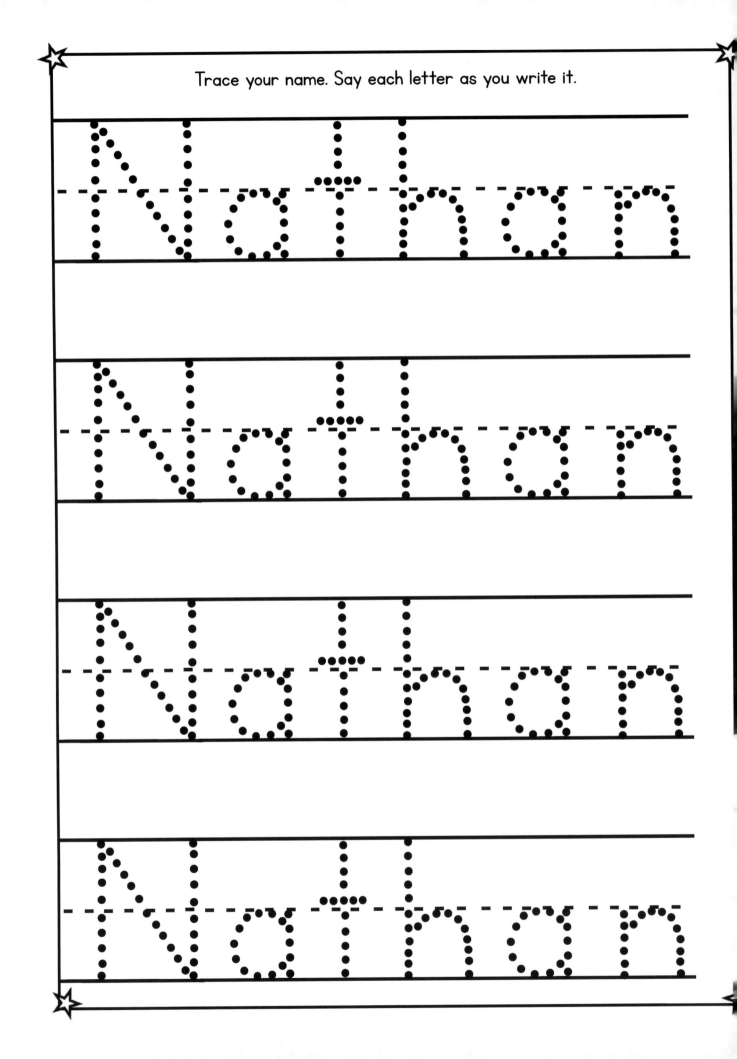

Trace your name. Say each letter as you write it.

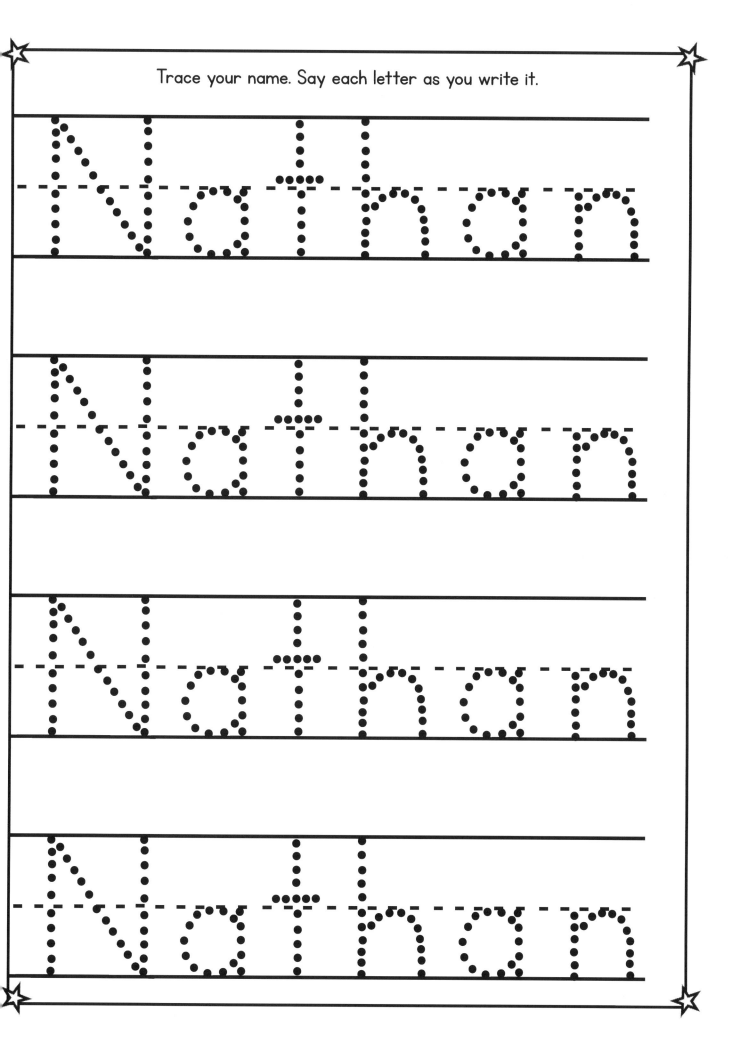

Trace your name. Say each letter as you write it.

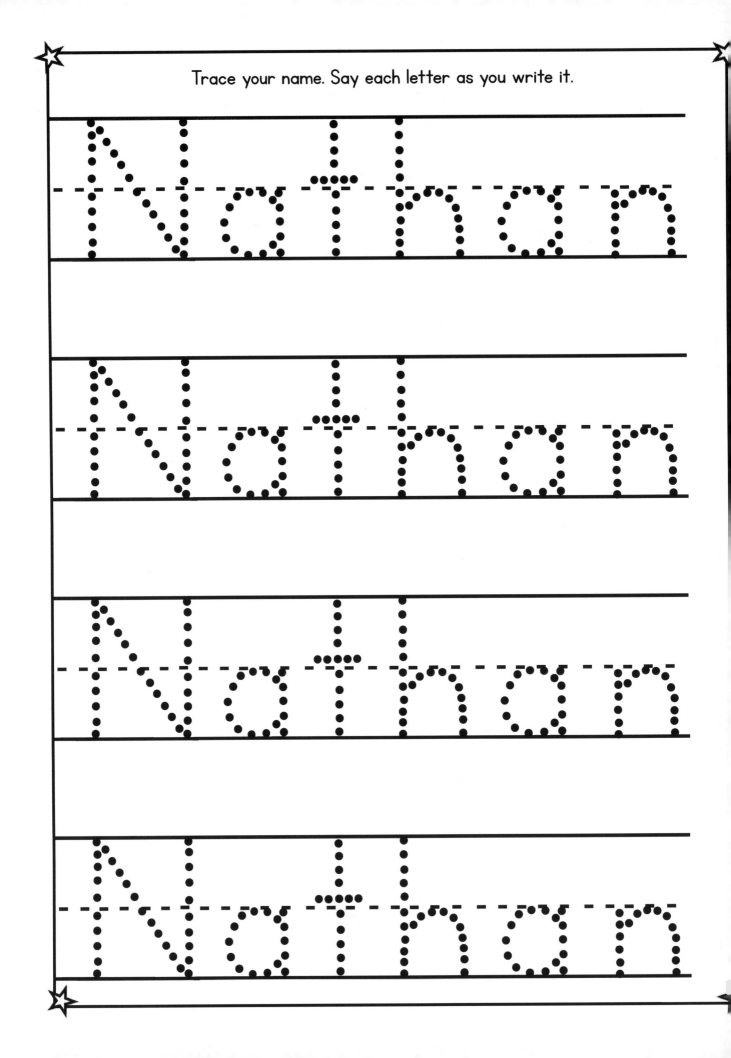

Trace your name. Say each letter as you write it.

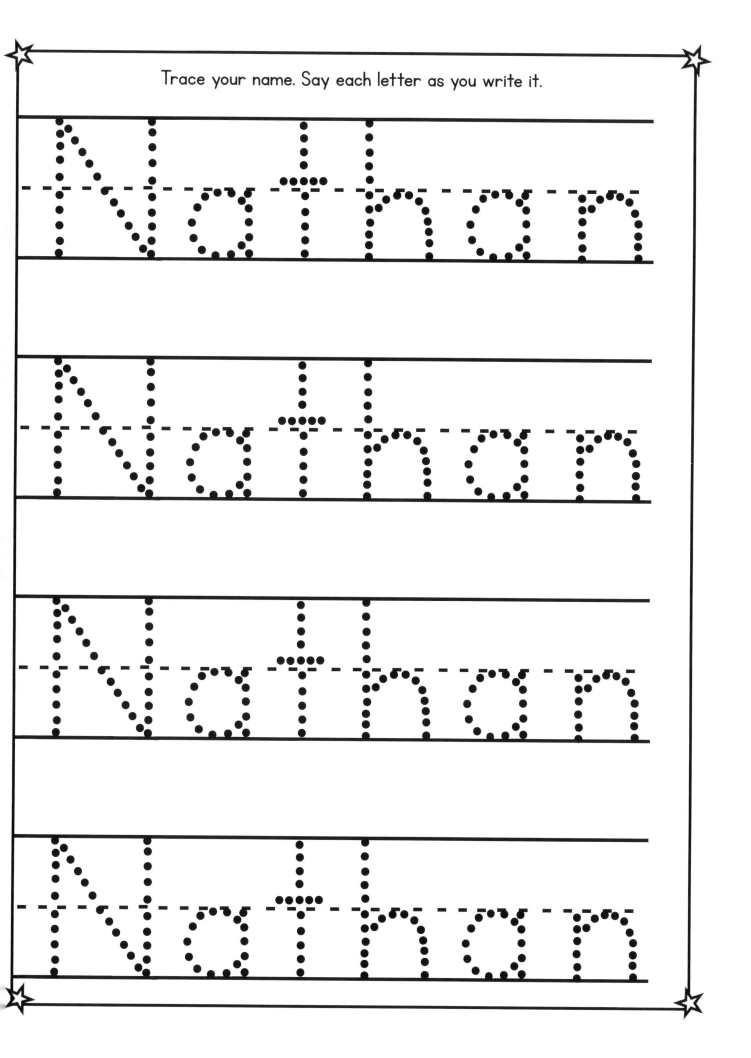

Write the missing letters in your name.

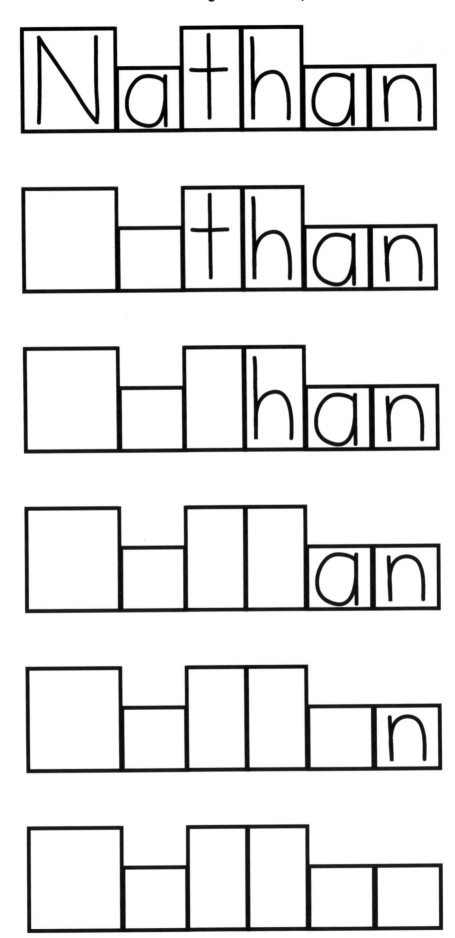

Write the missing letters in your name.

Nathan

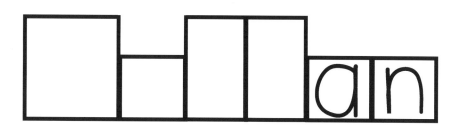

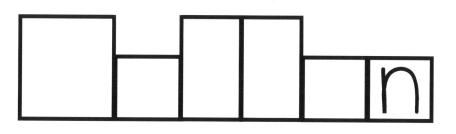

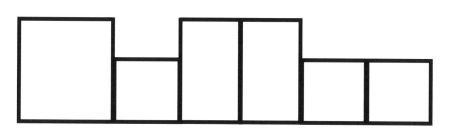

Write the missing letters in your name.

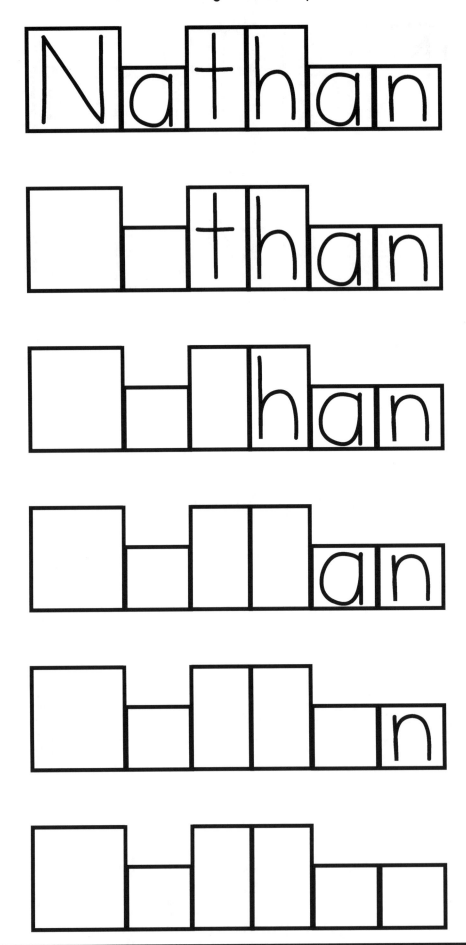

Write the missing letters in your name.

Nathan

_ _ t h a n

_ _ _ h a n

_ _ _ _ a n

_ _ _ _ _ n

_ _ _ _ _ _

Write the missing letters in your name.

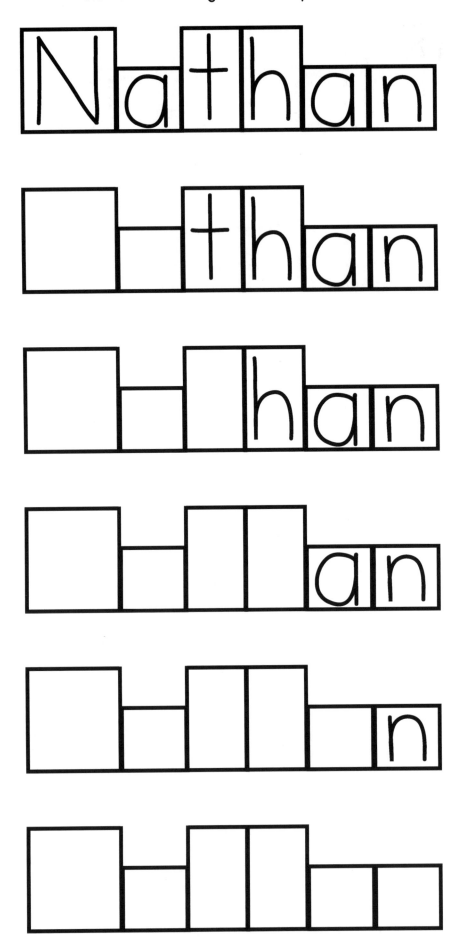

Write the missing letters in your name.

Nathan

_ _ than

_ _ _ han

_ _ _ _ an

_ _ _ _ _ n

_ _ _ _ _ _

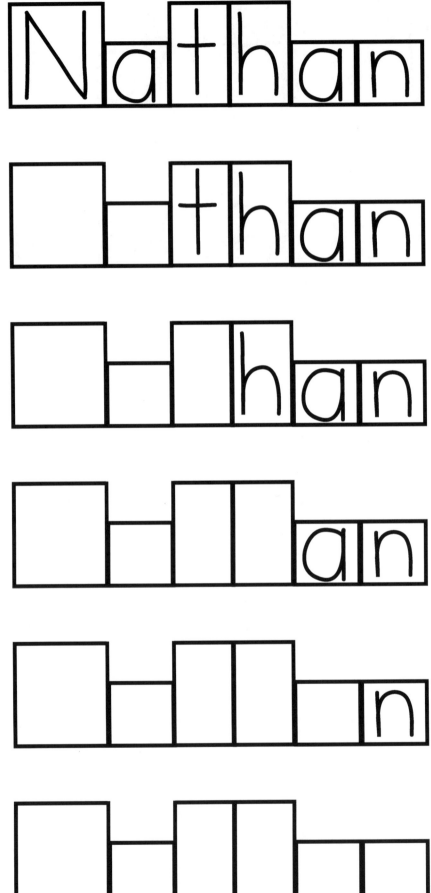

Write your name. Try using different colors!

Nathan

Nathan

Nathan

Nathan

Write your name. Try using different colors!

Nathan

Nathan

Nathan

Nathan

Write your name. Try using different colors!

Nathan

Nathan

Nathan

Nathan

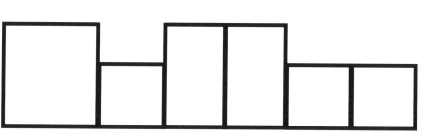

Write your name. Try using different colors!

Nathan

Nathan

Nathan

Nathan

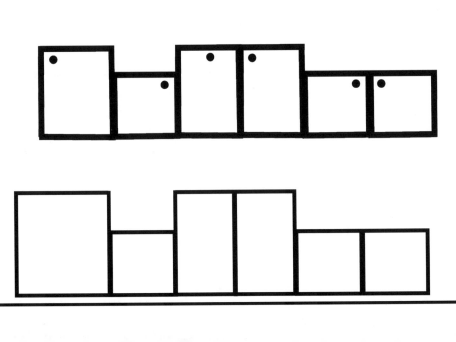

Write your name. Try using different colors!

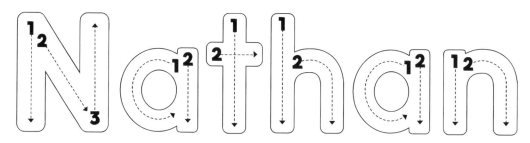

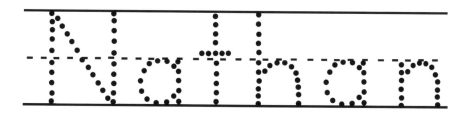

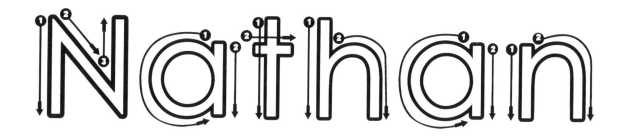

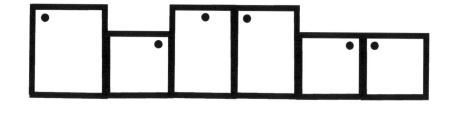

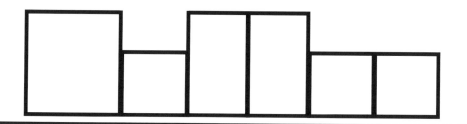

Write your name. Try using different colors!

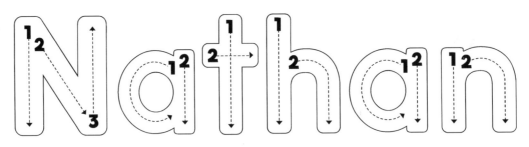

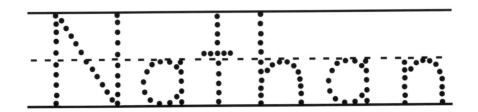

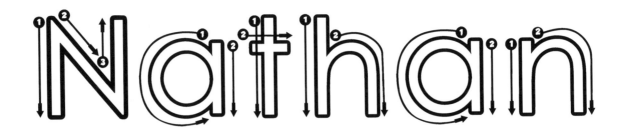

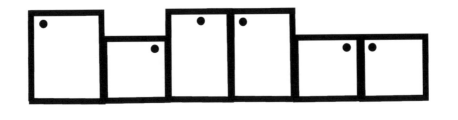

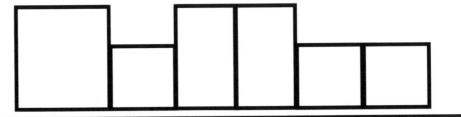

Write your name. Try using different colors!

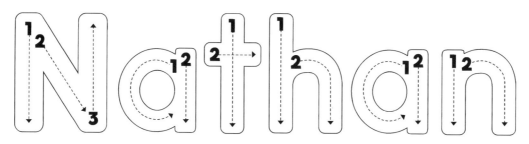

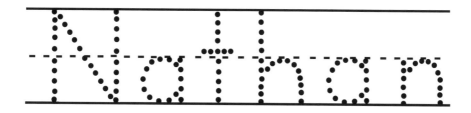

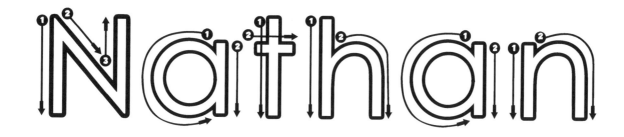

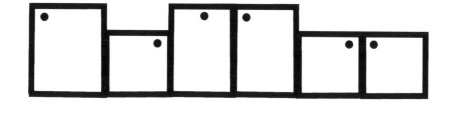

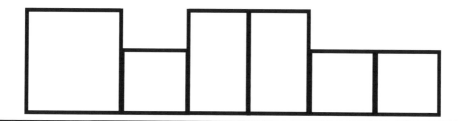

Write your name in the boxes. Use the dot as the starting point for each letter in your name.

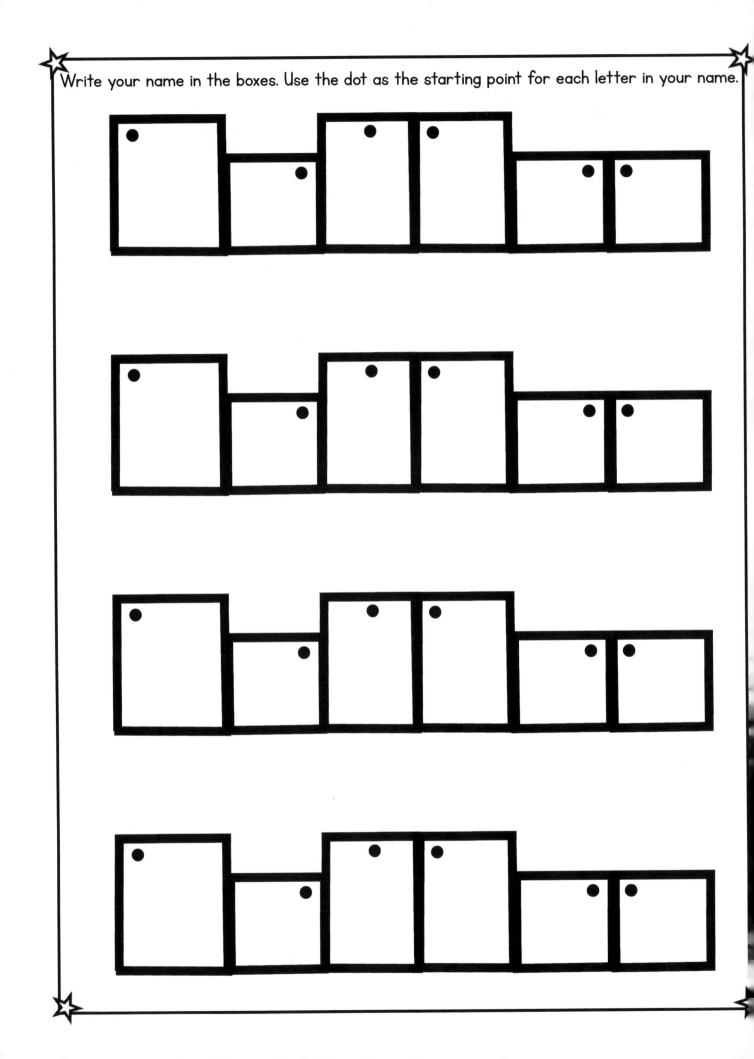

Write your name in the boxes. Use the dot as the starting point for each letter in your name.

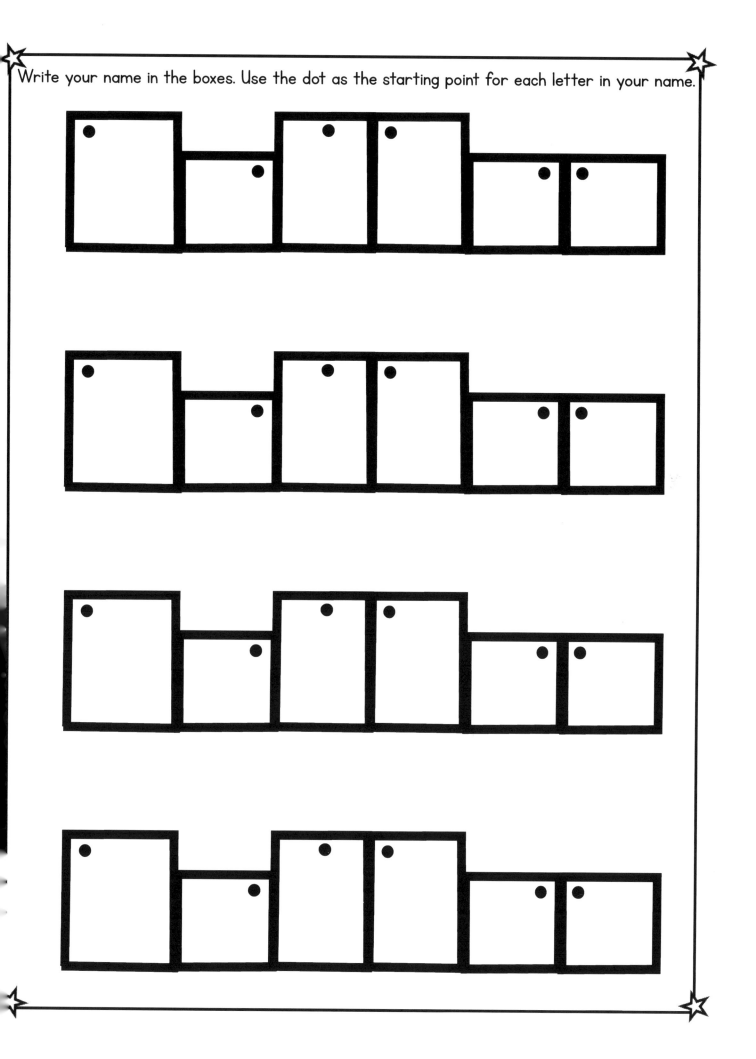

Write your name in the boxes. Use the dot as the starting point for each letter in your name.

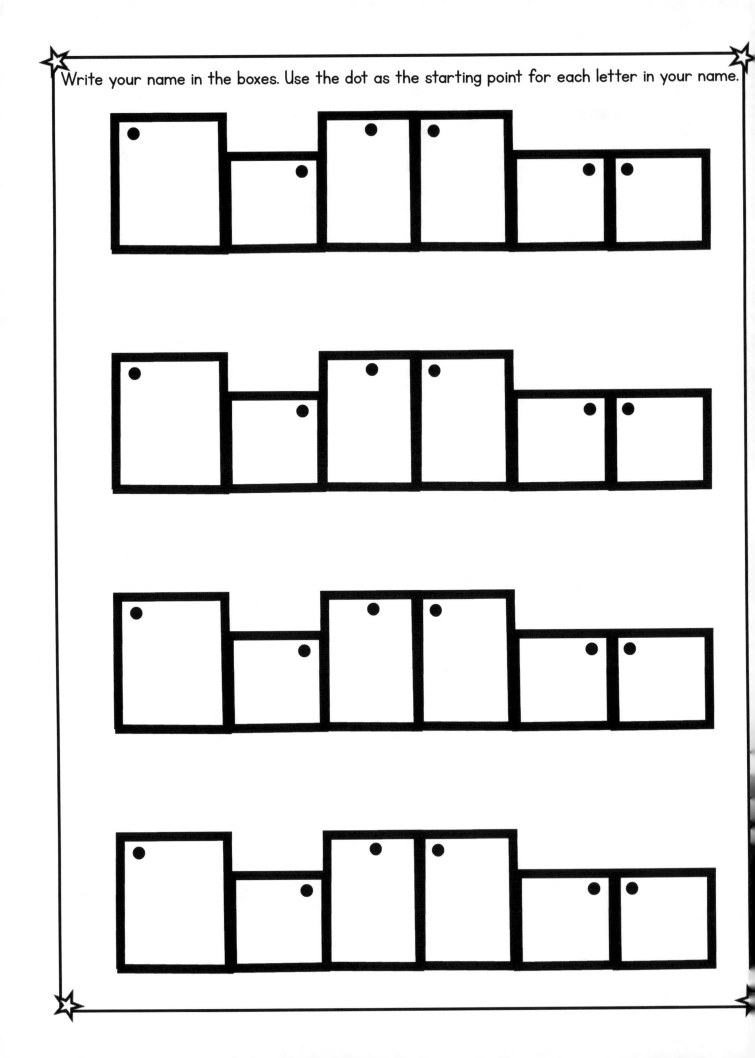

Write your name in the boxes. Use the dot as the starting point for each letter in your name.

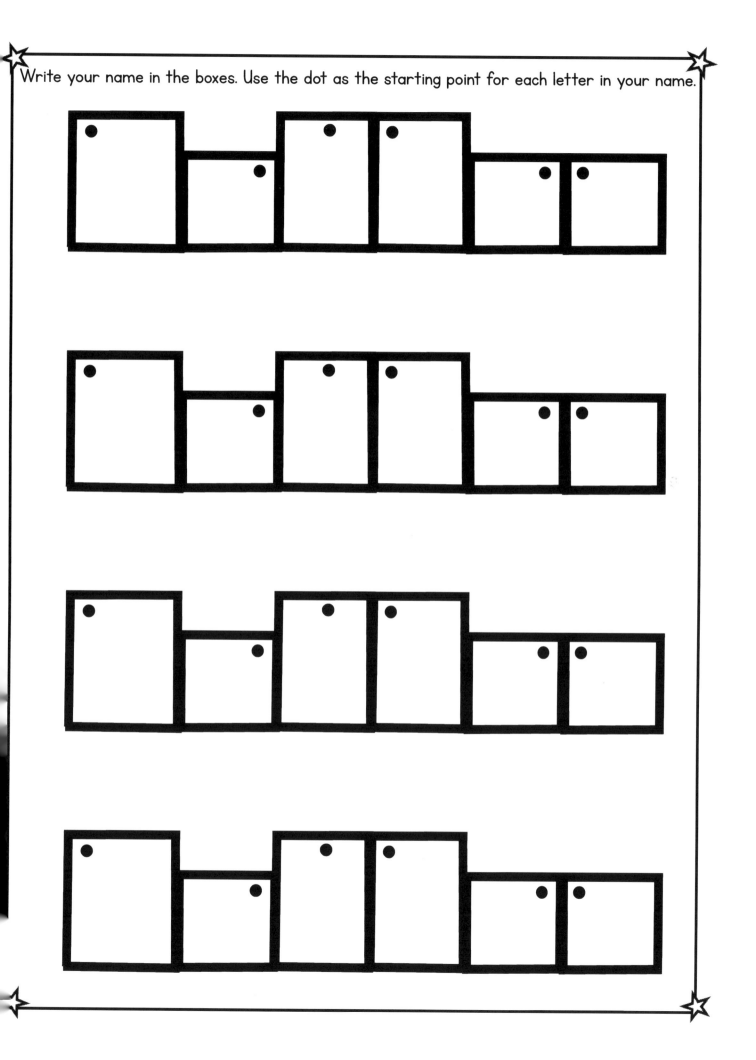

Write your name in the boxes. Use the dot as the starting point for each letter in your name.

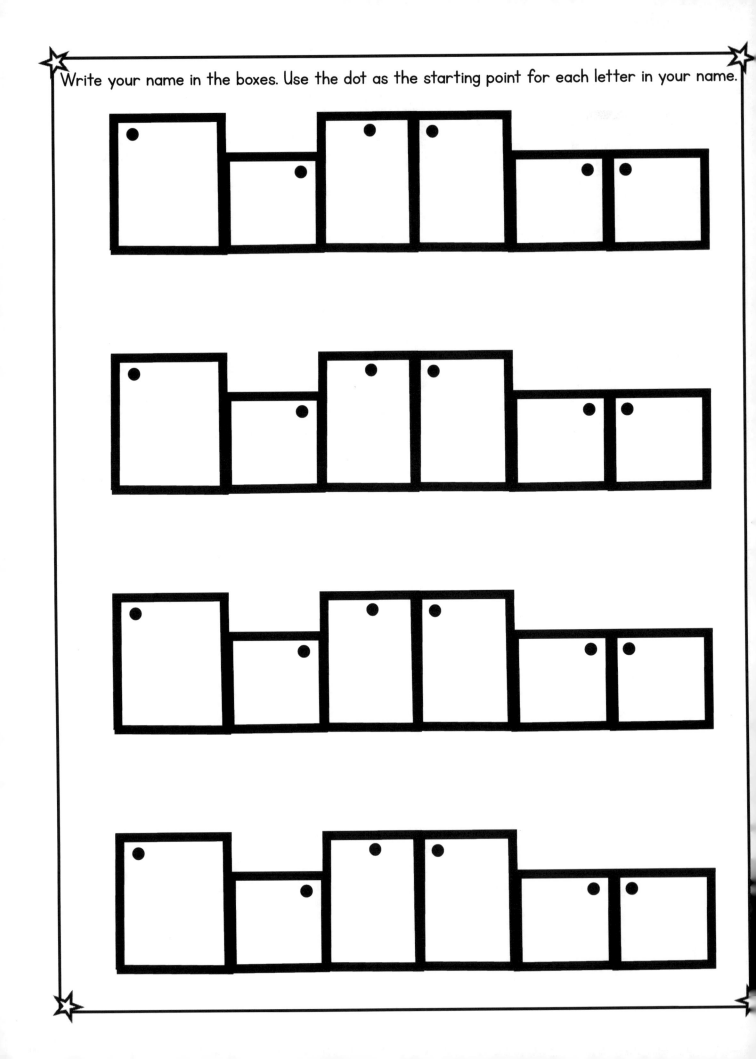

Write your name in the boxes. Use the dot as the starting point for each letter in your name.

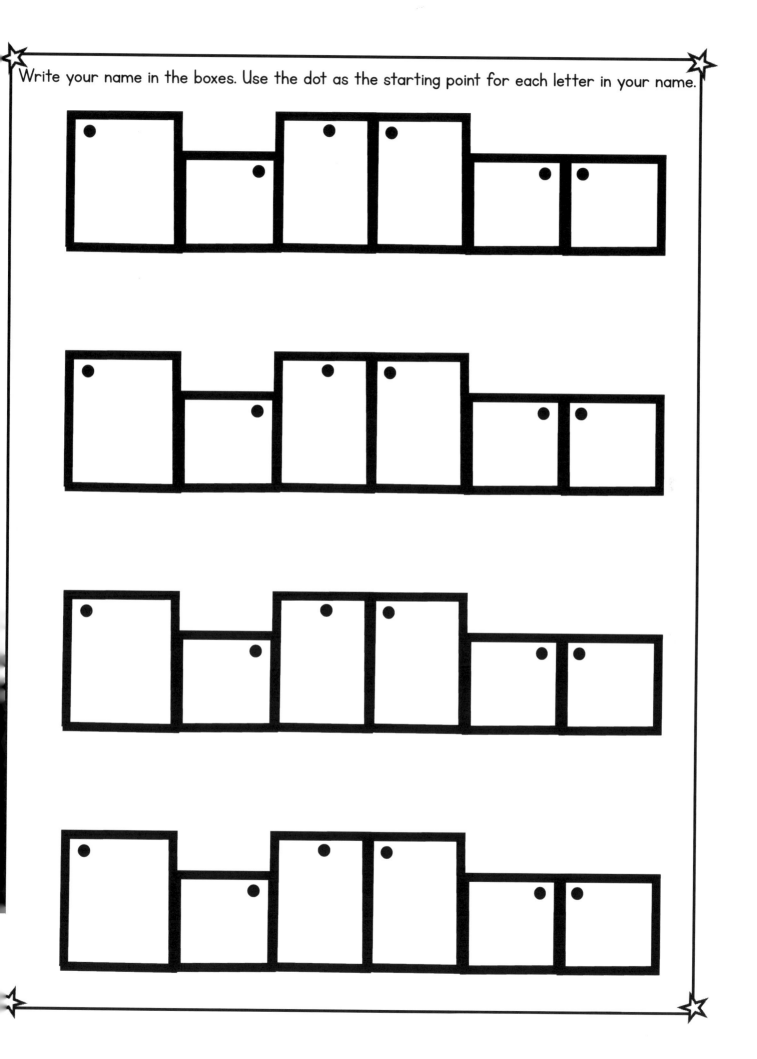

Write your name in the boxes. Use the dot as the starting point for each letter in your name.

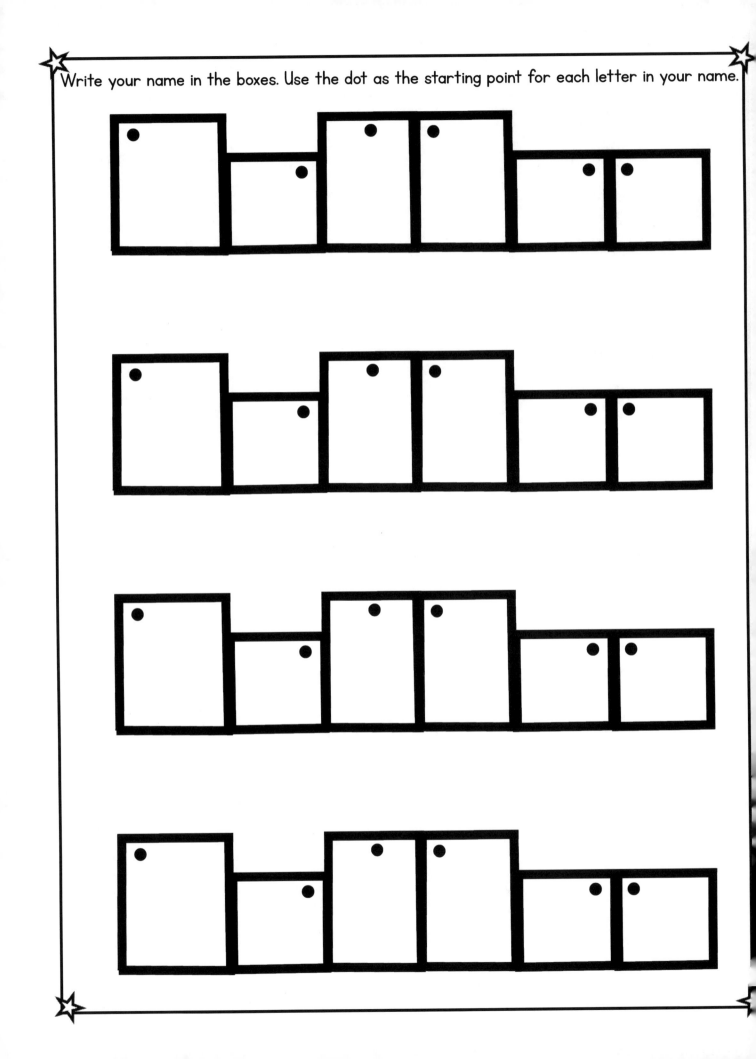

Write each letter of your name in a box.

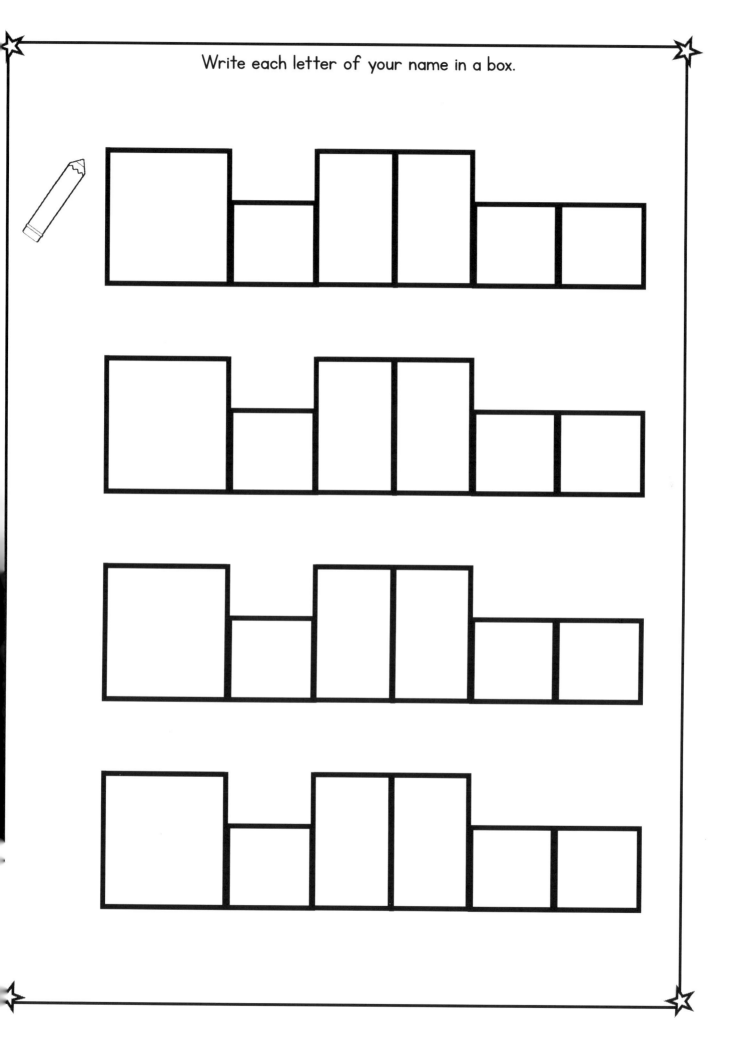

Write each letter of your name in a box.

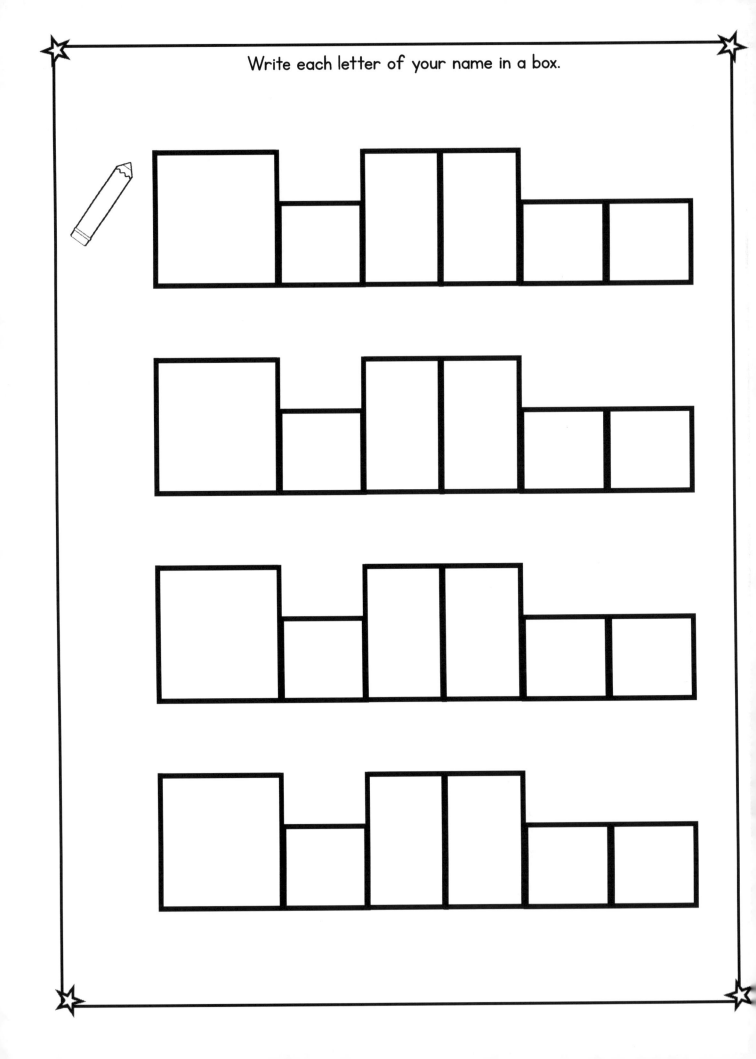

Write each letter of your name in a box.

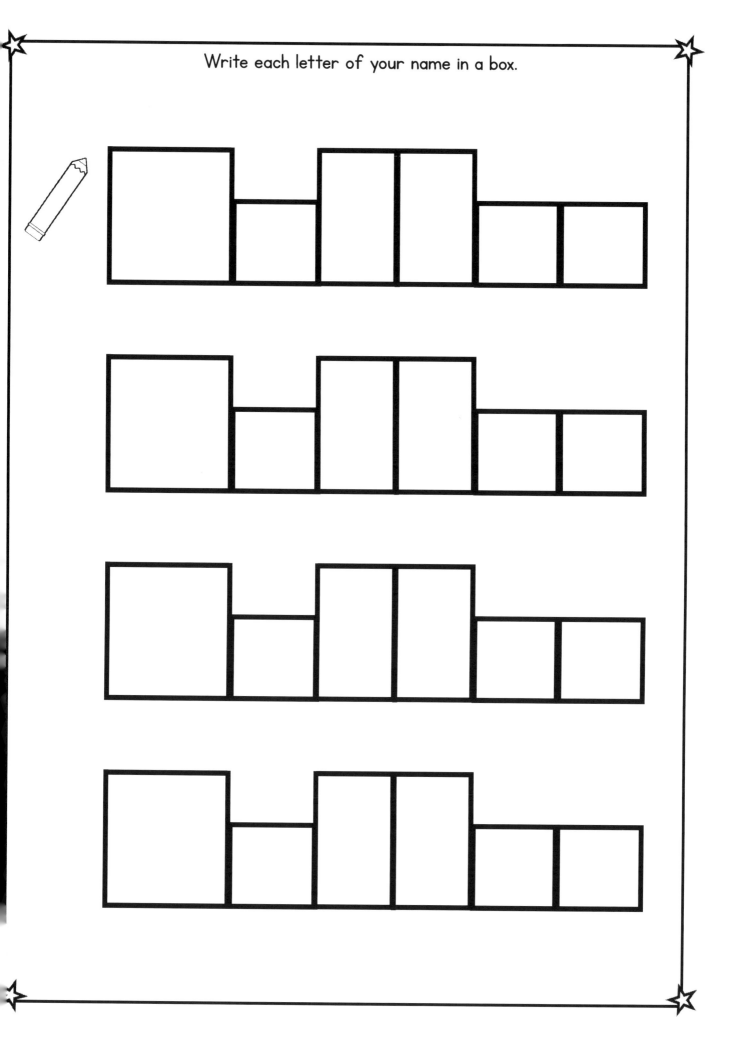

Write each letter of your name in a box.

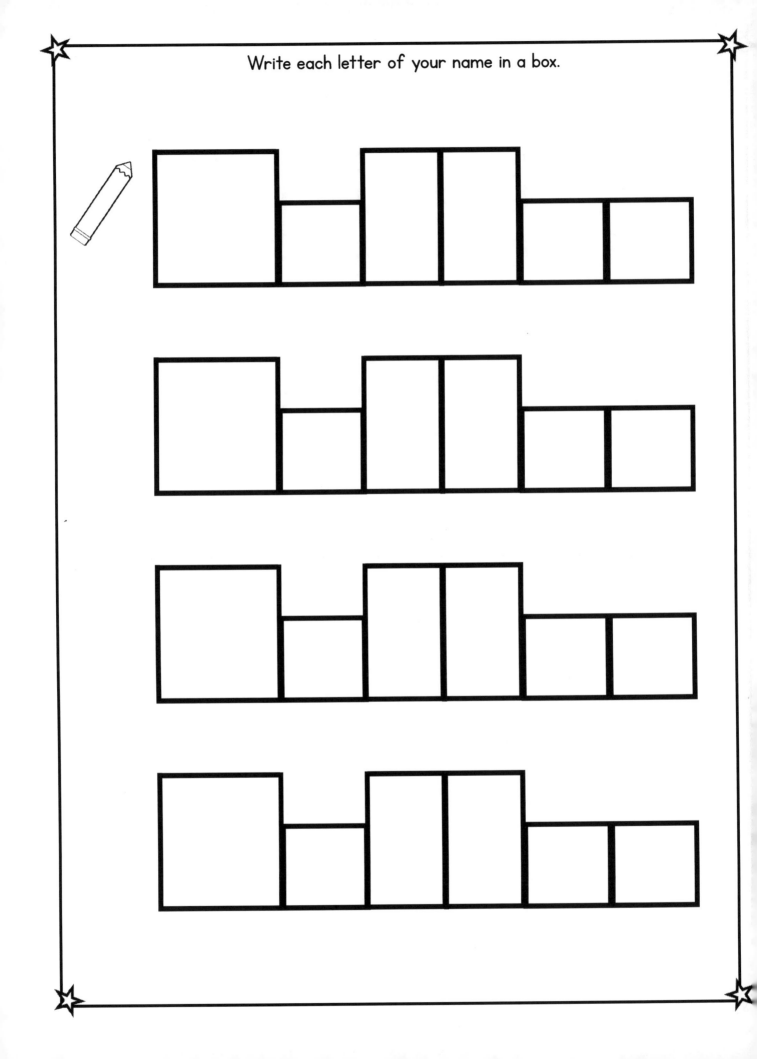

Write each letter of your name in a box.

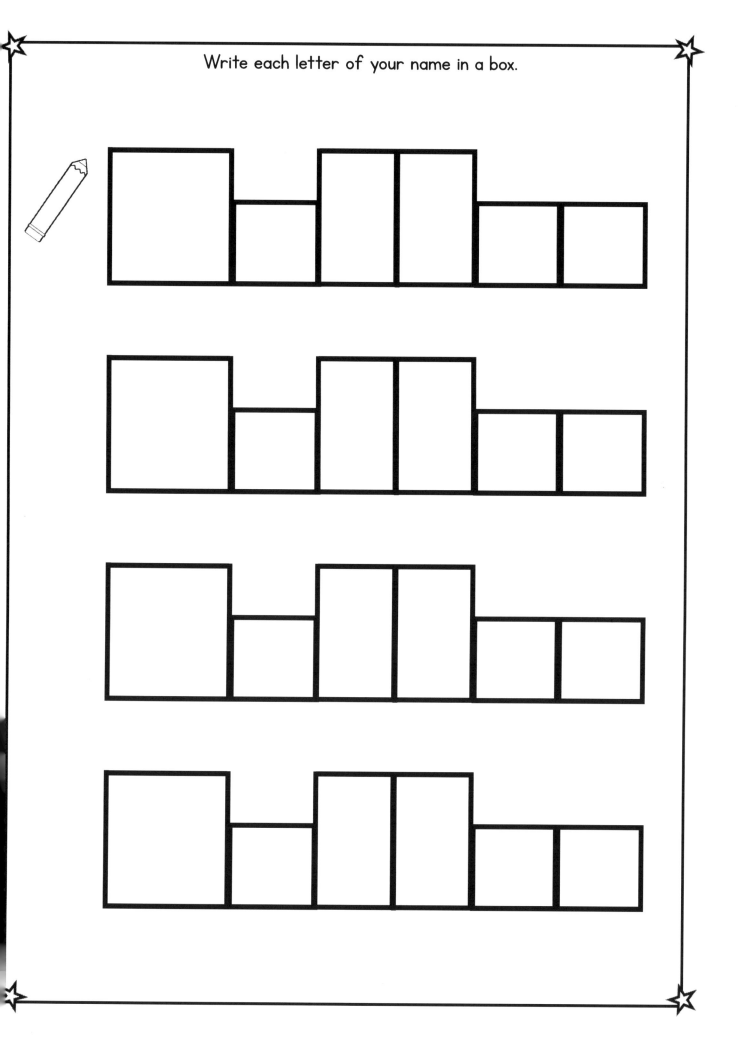

Write each letter of your name in a box.

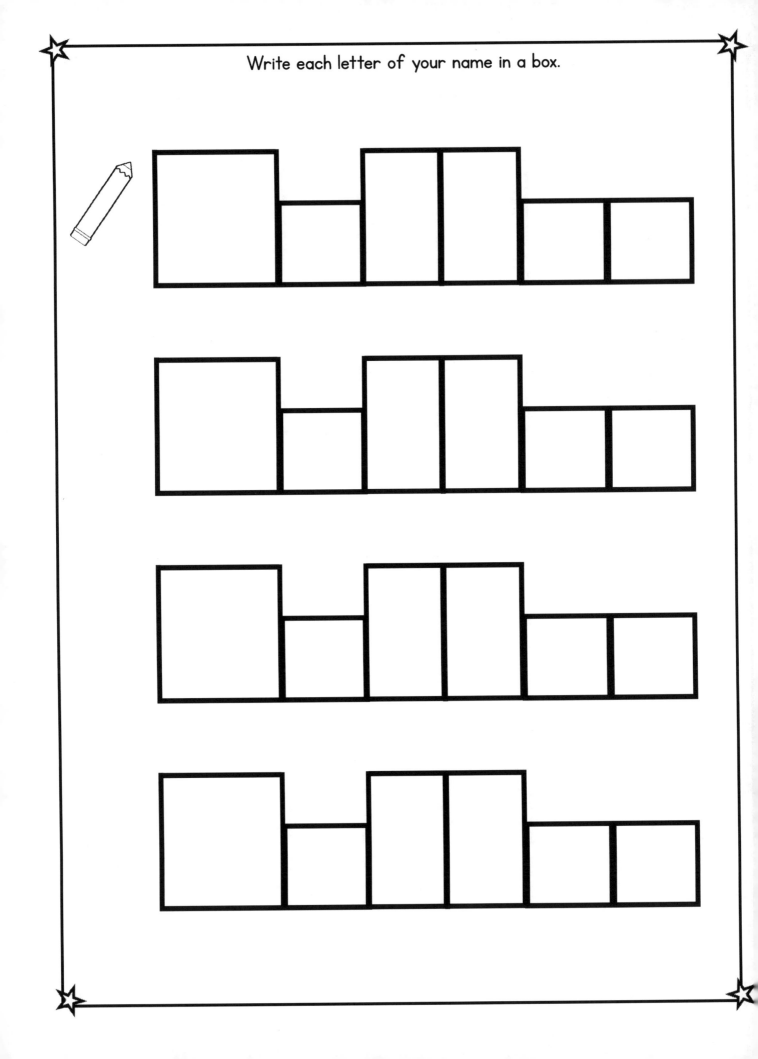

Write each letter of your name in a box.

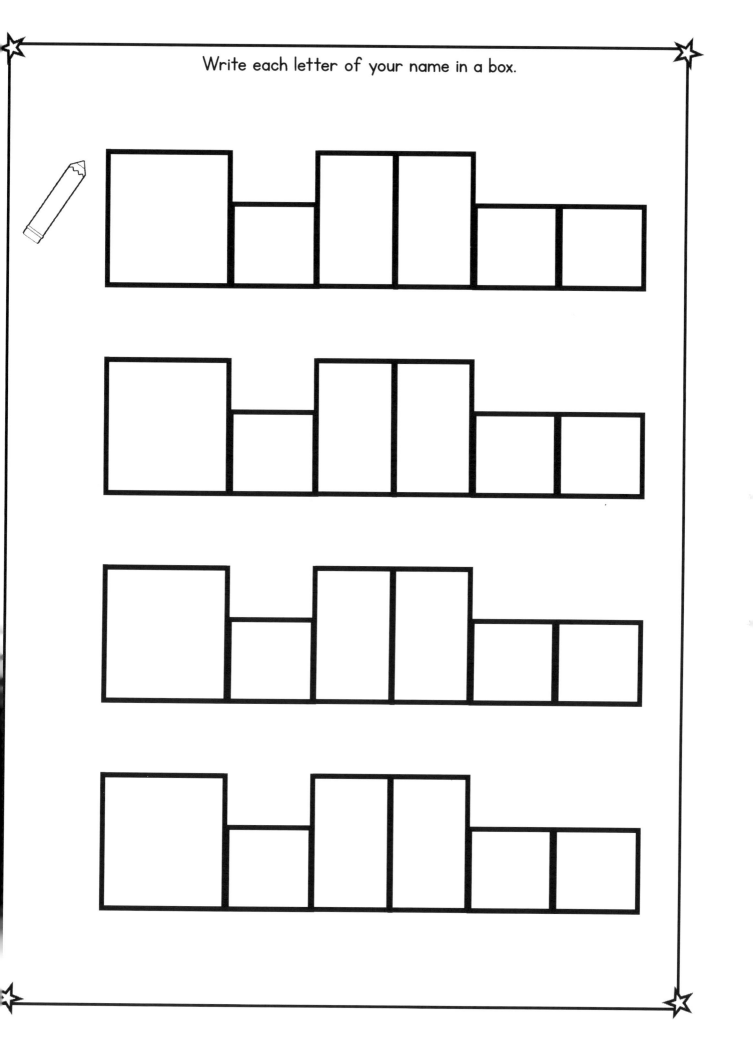

Nathan

Practice writing your name on the lines below.

Nathan

Practice writing your name on the lines below.

Nathan

Practice writing your name on the lines below.

Nathan

Practice writing your name on the lines below.

Nathan

Practice writing your name on the lines below.

Practice writing your name on the lines below.

Practice writing your name on the lines below.

Practice writing your name on the lines below.

Practice writing your name on the lines below.

Practice writing your name on the lines below.

Practice writing your name on the lines below.

Practice writing your name on the lines below.

My name is
_____

My name is
_____

My name is

My name is

Congratulations,

Nathan

on learning how to write your awesome name!

Now learn how to write all the uppercase and lowercase letters on the following pages!

Uppercase Letters

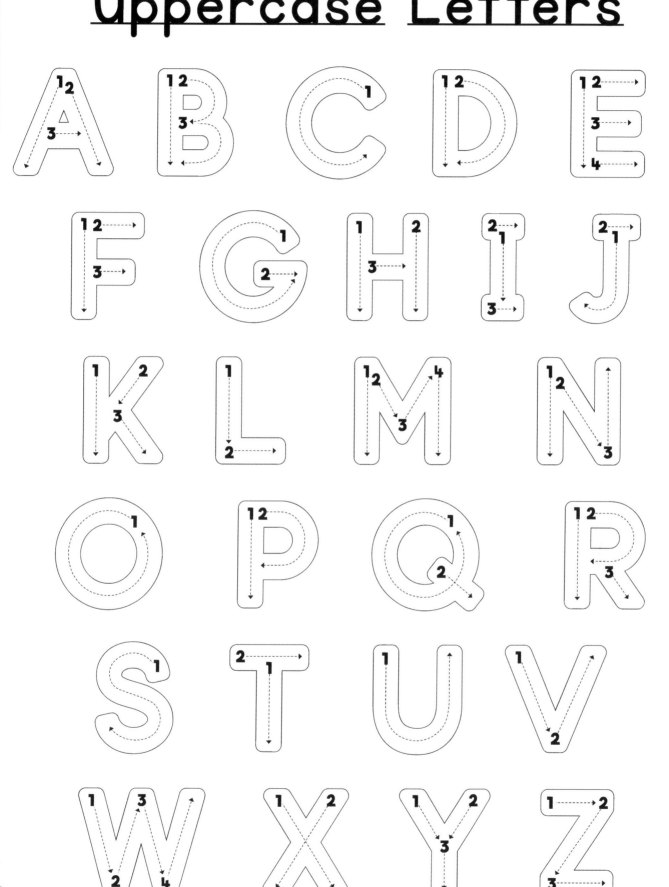

<u>Lowercase</u> <u>Letters</u>

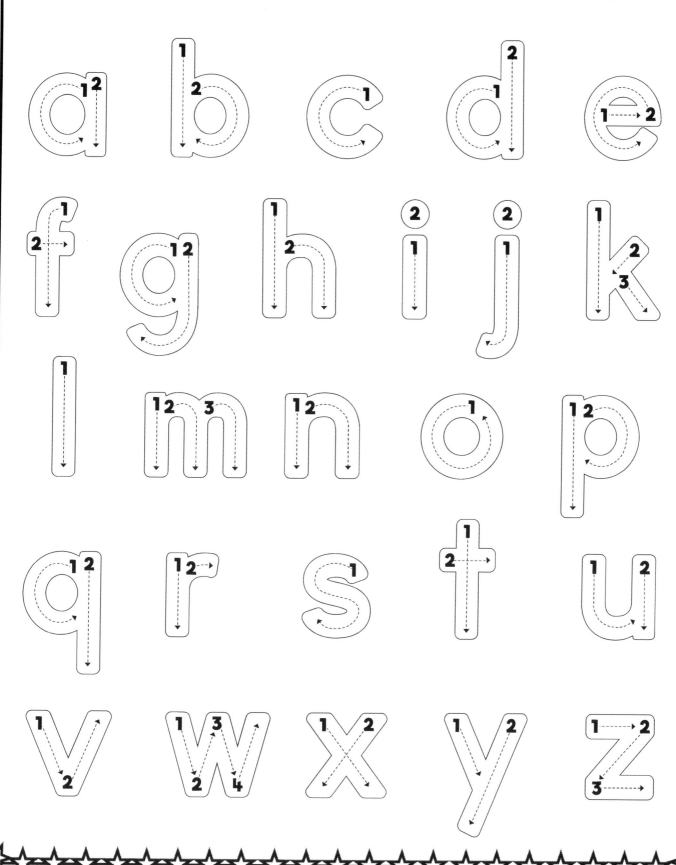

If you enjoyed this book, kindly leave a review on Amazon and check out Kids Print Hub on Amazon for more books.
Your feedback is greatly appreciated.

If you are looking for another book like this with a specific first name, middle name, or last name that is not on Amazon.com please email kidsprinthub@gmail.com with "My name is" in the subject line and let us know the name you would like to see printed.

Thank you!

Made in the USA
Columbia, SC
21 May 2024

35887778R00046